892
1/

248
.4

Doherty, Catherine de Haueck

DOH Molchanie _ The Silence Of God

WITHDRAWN

MOLCHANIE
The Silence of God

MOLCHANIE
THE SILENCE OF GOD

✽ *Catherine de Hueck Doherty*

CROSSROAD · NEW YORK

1982
The Crossroad Publishing Company
575 Lexington Avenue, New York, NY 10022

Printed in the United States of America

Library of Congress Cataloging in Publication Data

Doherty, Catherine de Hueck, 1900–
    Molchanie: the silence of God.

    1. Spiritual life.   2. Silence.   I. Title.
BV4501.2.D596   248.4   81–17281
ISBN 0–8245–0407–0   AACR2

✳Contents

MOLCHANIE
The Silence of God

Silence

Silence
Is a dark night
Where first
The soul
Meets its death to self.

        Where noise
        Cannot abide
        Not noise of word
        But thoughts.

                Silence is a school
                Of Love and death
                That leads to
                Light.

Silence
Is a dark night
Where
Soul and mind
Abide
To wait
For light
That is God's Speech.

Silence
Is a school of
Love and death
Where soul
Meets life.

Silence
Is the key
To the immense
Furnace of Love—
The heart of
God.

Silence is
Speech
Of passionate love
Spent
In the arms of God.

Silence
Is—
One-ness
With the Lord!

10

✳ The Perils of the Sea of Silence

The aim of this book is to describe the silence of God. "Molchanie" means "silence," and "molchanik" means "a person who is silent." When I wrote *Poustinia, Sobornost,* and *Strannik,** I described a journey. One had to go first into the poustinia of the heart to allow God to cleanse oneself thoroughly, that is, cleanse one's soul of all that is not God. The soul having been cleansed becomes one with God, a sobornost. And then, one day, the Lord will tap your shoulder and say, "Now is the time to go on a pilgrimage, into the sea of silence."

Some people may *begin* their journey within the silence of God. God so attracts their hearts that they cannot resist. They allow him to enter their hearts and make his abode there. To these few, God reveals his silence at an early stage. But very few have this experience, which is like being hit with lightning. Most people must go through the three stages in their walk with God.

On this pilgrimage they must walk through a desert where the nights are cold and the days unbearably

*All available from Ave Maria Press.

11

hot, where there are all sorts of strange insects and animals. Imagery, you say! Yes, but who can describe what happens to people who spend a long, long time in a desert?

Then, as they pilgrimage, the Lord leads them slowly towards the sea of silence. From a silvery beach he bids them plunge into his immense silence. You enter this sea, it covers you, but you don't drown; the Lord does not want anyone to drown. With a profound faith you allow yourself to sink gently into this sea of silence.

This is an unusual sea. It is a sea in which a person, as he continues to descend, loses all fears—the fear of death, the fear of God. And now, in this infinite sea into which man has plunged out of love, he discovers Love. This silvery beach and the desert were portals to the sea of silence. Those who are called must enter. It is not yet the parousia. Oh, no! It is truly God's embrace of love, but it is also his embrace of trial. Because now, when you enter that immensity of silence, you will meet loneliness and rejection.

Have you ever seen loneliness? It has a thousand faces; it is never the same. It becomes your companion in the sea of silence, God's infinite sea of loneliness. It will never leave you. It might disappear for a moment or two, but it will return. Because the loneliness at your side is the loneliness of Christ.

Can you endure the utter loneliness of Christ? Consider the loneliness at the time of the Annunciation, when the Spirit overshadowed Mary, and the Child began to grow in her womb. Consider the loneliness of the Child and the Youth in St. Joseph's workshop. Then, his departure from home and his lonely walks throughout Palestine. Now you are beginning to understand his utter loneliness.

Finally, his silence before Pilate and his loneliness on the cross. When you stand beneath the cross, you will see loneliness itself. It will have a face, and it will look into your eyes. If you have reached the foot of the cross in your silence, then you have begun to understand the loneliness of Christ. One cannot understand the sea of silence unless one also understands the loneliness of Christ.

So prepare yourself. For you will begin to understand that this loneliness is only another way that God the Trinity uses to purify your soul. You see, the Trinity dwells within you—Father, Son, and Holy Spirit. From within your heart and soul they will breathe forth the infinite power which is their life. But for this to happen, the soul must be totally pure and ready to accept loneliness.

When we reach the silver sands and plunge into the great sea of God's silence, we begin to understand that he alone is God—Lover, Friend, the totality of gentleness, peace, and rest. He calls us and we cannot resist that call. We have to be alone with him. It is a necessity, it is a hunger. It has been said that prayer is a hunger. But this Christ walks with loneliness and rejection, and so must we.

Yes, rejection was also the constant companion of Christ. It walked with him from the moment of his conception until the moment of his resurrection.

While he was on earth, his words were often rejected. A few of his disciples received his words, but these words were rejected by the elders of the Jewish faith, by the High Priest. They were rejected by many of the people he loved. When they saw him on the cross, many lost all faith and hope in him. Oh, there were a few women there; there was St. John. There were some Romans who *had* to be there. That was the sum total of the entourage of the Great King. Yes, he walked in the shadow of rejection all his life.

We do not take rejection easily. We fight against it. In fact, we are ready to leave the silvery beach, the sea of silence, everything, because deep down somewhere in our hearts arises the reaction to rejection—anger. It is devilish and a fruit of the devil.

Anger is the opposite of peace, and peace is what the person lives by who has entered the sea of silence. In the arena of the soul a new struggle begins between peace and anger. God has permitted it; he alone knows when it will end. Anger is like a gem-laden ornament we grab that suddenly turns into a thousand snakes. That is what anger is, snakes that well up from the bottom of our souls to bite, to hurt, to kill.

Christ accepted rejection and forgave those who rejected him. We don't. The snakelike creatures that form deep down in our souls prevent us from forgiving. In the sea of God's silence, which is the baptismal water of Jesus Christ, we must forgive everyone so as to overcome the snakes of anger and hatred. This forgiveness will be a crucifixion, but it doesn't matter. Christ prayed for those who hurt him; so did the saints, and so must we.

If we love God, we shall be able to look upon rejection as a great blessing. Christ will share with us this excruciating pain and through it teach us how to love our enemies. All this we will learn in the sea of silence.

Within the infinite depths into which you plunge out

of love, this teaching will continue. You will absorb the lessons of pure, total love, a love that knows no bounds. You will understand how to love your enemies. Yes, and the anger that so often welled up within you will slowly, slowly vanish in the deep waters of the Lord's sea. You will know anger no more. Loneliness and rejection will continue to be your companions. You will be lonely and rejected as Christ was, with all the accompanying tragedy and terribleness. You may even be rejected by your friends, and certainly by your enemies.

When I first came to North America I didn't have any friends, but I had many enemies. People rejected me because to them I was just another "Polack." I leave it to your imagination how a foreign-born person lives with rejection. Only by the grace of God—but, oh, what a grace!

Oh, beloved, praise the Lord with me—loudly! Rejection is a great gift of his love! Can you imagine what Jesus Christ becomes to those who are rejected like he was? We share in his rejection. Dance! Let the music sound! The Son of God was totally rejected. Where is our place, the place of those who profess to love him? On the other side of his cross.

But do you know what happens when you accept rejection? A very simple thing. Our Lord takes you off the other side of his cross, tenderly kisses you, puts you in the arms of his mother, and bids her to be the Good Samaritan who pours oil over your wounds. She takes you home and consoles you. Now you know, as few people know, two things: the kiss of Christ, and the nursing love of his own mother. What more could we possibly desire?

In the poustinia, then, God cleanses the soul from everything that is extraneous to himself. It leads eventually to union with him, but this union is not yet complete. It will be complete when the soul that loves him so passionately is willing to enter the silence of God.

Don't think that those who enter the silence of God are "silent." Nothing could be farther from the truth! Molchanie is a thunder! You will be able to hear it everywhere. Your nights and days will be filled with it. You will be able to hear nothing but the thunder of God's silence.

Those whom God calls into his silence will enter a vortex which will shatter them into little pieces. Looking here and there you will see fragments of a human being. You will behold your own fragmentation and wonder why you do not die. I do not know why. God knows. But in his silence he will gather together your fragments. And when you emerge from the sea of silence you will be a thunder. And this thunder will pass beyond the galaxies as if you were a bird sent forth to preach the gospel to the whole universe.

Many confuse silence with *solitude*. Solitude is something quite different from silence. Solitude is being alone with God, waiting for God. But silence is an immense sea into which you enter and never leave. And once you have plunged into this silence, you will always be silent.

So don't mistake silence for solitude. Silence does not depend on your being alone. Whether you are in a streetcar, or in a church, teaching a class, or working as a typist, you can still be immersed in the silence of God. If you are immersed in this silence, the little things you do— scrub floors, wash carrots, work on a farm or in an office

—will be a thunder that spans the divide between sun and moon.

You do not realize it yet, but the preaching of the gospel emanates from the poustinia, creates a unity with God, then causes a confrontation with the world. You may be martyred, but, like a phoenix, you will arise again and again; like Christ, you will arise from a crucifixion *by people.*

Oh, they are not going to crucify you with nails and hammers. Oh, no! They will crucify you with words, with mockery: "Look, he believes in God, he believes that Christ is divine!" This will be worse than being crucified. But you will endure it. For the great silence of God will become a thunder all around you. People will not know where the thunder is coming from, but it will be coming from your heart. God has entered it through his silence. Having put together your fragmented self, he now tells you to go on a pilgrimage to preach his gospel in a silence that is more powerful than any words you have ever spoken. Yes, of such elements is silence made.

Silence is more powerful than any words, except one: the Word. It is by entering the Word that to some the gift of utter silence, and therefore complete speech, is given.

But silence has another dimension that doesn't belong to the Word. Silence does not necessarily lead to peace and closeness to God. No! It can also be a temptation. One must understand this temptation of silence because it comes from the Tempter himself. He is allowed to tempt us by a false silence, so that we might discover what true silence is. I will give you a few examples.

You can barely hear the water that some slave is pouring over Pilate's hands. That was done in utter silence.

The Jews and Romans listened with bated breath to that dead sound of water that was no sound at all. Many stood there and allowed this false silence to enter their hearts. Some, I am sure, wrapped their cloaks around themselves and walked away. This silence—this silence of injustice—was unbearable.

There is the silence of a cruel death. I remember that when my husband and I were starving in Finland (I have described this in other books), silence was all around us. But it wasn't the silence of God. It was the silence of the Tempter. My husband and I went to sleep; there was nothing else to do. There was good, fresh water, but water alone does not sustain you for long.

So we went to sleep. Don't ever try to find silence in the escape of sleep, unless you are really sick and you can sleep in a sort of emotional vacuum. Otherwise, don't. Take it from me. That when you are hungry, and you go to sleep to find silence, silence finds you. But it isn't the silence of God. It is the silence of the Tempter, who laughs in your face and presents you with many tempting dishes.

We went to sleep. I don't know what my husband dreamt about, but I dreamt of succulent meats, lovely salads, the beautiful cold melons so beloved by the Russians. And when we woke up and tried to orient ourselves, it seemed as if we heard in the distance a diabolical laughter. For he had finished with us, or so he thought, had left us in the utter silence of his living hell, and he was content.

But God had other plans! We were saved from the hellish silence.

You wish to experience this kind of silence? Go into

the alleyways of the world. Look at the garbage pails and see the old ladies rummaging through them, and the children collecting what you have thrown away. The poor go about this task in silence, a despairing silence, crying silently to God. People have closed their hearts to these poor. So some day, when you have nothing to do, walk through the garbage alleys of the world. Then you will know the silence of the Devil. And in that silence two thoughts will emerge: "Will I share more with the poor?" and "To hell with the poor!" What effect will this silence have on *you*?

Silence can lead us to God, and that is why the Evil One constantly tries to interfere with it. Take, for instance, the silence of indifference.

Silence

Silence is a wall
Made of black,
And coiled stone
Like a snake

> Immovable
> Inscrutable
> Silence has stood
> Cool
> Aloof
> Wall without a roof!

Men have hurled
Bodies and souls
Against
Its blackness
Hardness
And have died trying!

> Bodies and
> Souls
> Broken and dead
> Lie at the foot
> Of the black
> And cold stone
> Silence is . . .
> Am I one of them?

There is a silence which doesn't say a single word, negative or positive. It's a silence whose very nature is to deny what it believes, or deny everything. How many people throughout the ages have entered into this silence! They didn't actually bear "false witness." They simply entered the silence of denial. They stood in front of those who questioned them and didn't say anything. They just stood there, mute witnesses to a tragic denial.

Perhaps in their ears echoed and re-echoed the words of Christ: "He who denies me before men, I will deny before my Father." Did these silent ones understand what they were doing? As one looks at the course of history, it becomes quite clear that there are many such silent ones. But what type of silence is it that does not refute, does not deny, that turns man into a stone? Peter denied God three times, but then he went out and wept when the cock crowed the third time. Do these people hear the voice of the cock?

I met a man in Russia once; he was about twenty-five or thirty. The Communists had questioned him about his belief in God. He became like a stone. In no way did he indicate whether he did or did not believe in God. The interrogation continued. I didn't hear all of it except the last sentence, when somebody said to him, "Will you deny your own God if you believed in him?" There was no answer. Perhaps I didn't hear the answer.

As I walked down the street (it happened on a street where members of the Red Army, who were half drunk, were, in a manner of speaking, teasing the man more than interrogating him) I realized that in our own century, a lot of us only professed to believe. Oh, we went to church. If we were Catholics we went to confession once a month. We attended the Easter services and things like that. But our deeds were opposed to our beliefs.

This sham belief is the reason for all the cults today. Youth walks the earth, silent searchers for the Absolute. They do not find the Absolute because the majority of believers have not entered God's silence but the silence of the Tempter. Only he can change a human being into a stone, so that the grace of the Lord cannot penetrate into him.

When I was small we were in Egypt. My parents took me to see the beautiful stone statues of the kings. My father was six-foot-two and a half, but even he looked like a pygmy in front of those huge statues of the Rameses.

Last night, in the dark warmth of Arizona, I couldn't sleep. Now, many years later, it seemed that my father was holding my hand and pointing out, not these huge statues, but a tragic forest of stonelike people who by their silence denied their beliefs.

I woke up with a great fear, almost a panic. I went to the little altar we had in the house and I prayed that these stone people might open up to receive the love of Christ. I again fell asleep. But throughout the night I knew that men were turning into a forest of stone. I also knew that man was free to say yes or no to this silence. I woke up. Once more I heard the voice of Christ, "He who denies me before men, I will deny him before my Father."

Come, then. Let us run hand in hand into the deep sea of silence. Let us run hand in hand into the devilish sea of rejection and loneliness, and laugh and laugh at the devil. He thinks this sea will drown us. He is wrong. Christ has conquered!

✳ Plunging into the Sea

J ust before plunging into this infinite sea of mystery and love, just before entering its depths, the soul is poised and reflective. It's as if God was addressing a question to the soul, and God stood there waiting for an answer: "What is your choice?" And God waits. Isn't it awesome that man can make God wait? But he does.

In rapid succession, memories of the soul's long pilgrimage pass before its eyes. The pilgrim's eyes are closed; he listens. And somewhere out of the past, out of the infinite silence which is the Lord's speech, he remembers the voice that called, "Come then, my love, my lovely one, come" (Song of Songs, 2,10). He remembers that at one time—he has almost forgotten when or where—he arose and followed that voice throughout a long, long pilgrimage, until he finally arrived at these silver sands where he stands now, deciding how to answer the question.

He stands now, face to face with God. He remembers how he started out in some poustinia, and saw the face of God there, but never saw it as much as he desired. Then God called him on a pilgrimage. Few people choose to go. He went through both untold hardships and untold delights, then finally arrived at the silver sands, where the waves were lapping on the shore.

And here God asks him the question: "Will you accept the new vocation of silence?" It is not the vocation of living alone. No. It is the vocation of entering the sea of infinity to preach the gospel in deep silence, and by preaching the gospel silently, drawing an innumerable host of people towards God.

The silver sands are so warm. The sun shines on them in a very special way. I stand there, and there are others around me, but not many. We are all looking at this beautiful shining, sun-reflecting sea, which during the night reflects the moon and the stars. It especially reflects the infinity of God.

It is time to plunge, yes, time to take the plunge into this deep and immense sea that is the infinity of God. There is no other sea like it. It is the sea of his Heart, and those who hunger and thirst to be alone with him are the ones invited into it. Listen! Hear the waves lapping on the shore. Each wave says, "Come, come, come." And we have to go. Not because we are impelled by any fear or by anything human. Oh, no! We are impelled by love, by a love that knows no bounds. Even if you are still bound, in a little while your love will be like Christ's—boundless. Like him, you will open your arms to embrace the whole world—all peoples, all races, even your enemies.

There is no hesitation now in our hearts. As we lift up our eyes it's as if God smiles down upon us. The next thing we know we are entering the warm waters of the sea, which are the waters of baptism made holy by the presence of Christ. Only now they have become this immense sea, which seems to cover everything, because God is infinite. And quite close to the ears of our souls we hear the voice of our God: "He who has given up everything for Me will receive a great reward."

How the sea beckons! See! We have already gone up to our knees. Now up to our waists. Now up to our necks. And then, like one who dives into a wave, we willingly plunge into the very depths, because he who loves us is in the depths. In time, we will be one with him, and the Christ in us will embrace the whole world.

Be at peace, be at peace. It is a time of waiting. Be very quiet, very quiet. For now we must hear the words of God coming from the depths. Listen very carefully! For here, out of the depths, he will begin to teach us how to become totally identified with himself.

The silver sands are gone. So is the mountain that was in the background. There is nothing now except water. Is it water, or is it the infinity of God's mercy and God's power? The step has been taken. Everything has been left behind. Nothing, nothing remains.

Those of us who have jumped into the infinite waters of God come out somewhere onto a shore that has no sand or mountains or sun. It is rough country. There are sharp stones, boulders, and knolls that seem part of a larger mountain whose summit cannot be seen. Are we supposed to walk over these sharp stones? Is it for this that we left the silver sands? Is it for this that we plunged heedlessly into the warm sea of God's mercy? The sharp stones barely form the outline of a path leading up somewhere. But the Voice whispers, as if from afar: "Come. I am waiting for you. Come."

And so, sharp stones or not, bare feet or not, we, the pilgrims of the Absolute, we who are searching for God with our whole beings, follow the barely visible path of silence. We did not know it would be so harsh. We did not know it would be so lonely. No matter. We have to go. The silence of God draws us on like a lover draws his beloved. It doesn't matter if we leave bloody footprints along the way. Nothing matters except the entry into God's silence. We have met his silence before, and the silence of the Devil and of indifference. We have understood a little bit—not much—of the loneliness of Christ and his rejection.

Now, as we slowly walk this stony path, which cuts the soles of our feet, from somewhere we hear the voice of the Tempter: "Turn back!" But we can't. We must go on to meet God. Suddenly we hear another voice, more clear and powerful than the first: "If any man is thirsty, let him come to me! Let him drink who believes in me" (Jn. 7:37–38).

We realize that *we* are the ones who are hungry and thirsty, and we are astonished that we have come so far in our following of Christ. We fall on our knees and cry out, "Lord, have mercy on me." Then, before our very eyes, Christ stands. In his hand is a cup of wine. In his other hand is a piece of Jewish flat bread. He hands me, and those who came with me, the chalice, which is a wooden cup. He tears the bread apart so that each of us has enough. We eat and drink, and then we fall asleep.

When we awake there is no bread and wine, but we are refreshed, and we now have the strength to move upward over the terrible stones, over the briers and thorns which try to hold us back. With a quiet, slow, firm pace we move forward. He who has received the bread and wine, food for the day, has been consoled by Christ.

As we move quietly and simply up the stony path, a new mystery is revealed to us. The consolation we have received we must pass on to others. This consolation is the Good News that God loves us. The faith, hope, and love of our hearts pass over into the hearts of others, and they are consoled.

Now we know why we followed Christ into such great silence: to experience how one grows strong in Christ by being fed by him. We understand also that our silence now covers the whole world, because it is not ours, but his.

Silence and Atonement

My heart
And I
Have
Learned
Silence
Today.

It took us
Very long
To understand
That silence
Is part
Of the domain
Of Lady Pain.

That there
Are courts
And stairs
And turrets
And chambers
Without end
In the domain
Of Lady Pain.

And that
My heart
And I
As we grow
Will
Surely and slowly know
(Because we
Are yet fairly
Small . . .
And not quite
Learned as
Yet in all
The ways
Of pain
And love)
Spend some
Time
In every court
And walk
Each steep
Step
Of every stair
And enter

Turrets
Chambers
One by one
And stay in
Each . . .
Until each
One
Has taught

My heart
And me
Its lesson
Of pain,
Its chant
Of love.

And then
Some day
We do
Not know when
My heart
And I . . .
Will
Find

The
Last
Strange
Ladder
That
Will
Bring us
To final
Ecstasy
And death
That starts
A life
Of endless
And eternal
Delight.

But that
Is not yet
For we
Must
Learn
To suffer
And to wait . . .
To hide
From all
The
Facts
That

Now
We live
In two
Domains
That of
Earth
And that of
Lady Pain.

We are
So slow
My heart
And I . . .
To learn
Anything
At all . . .
And yet
Today
We learned

The art
Of silence
When in pain.
We learned
That the skins
Of a white doe
Bind tight

And that
They increase
The pain
A hundredfold
Yet silence
Must be kept.
We tried
So hard
Today
When we
Were crucified.

And now we know
That pain
Born
For Love's
Sake
Is like
A flame
That brings
Us in
The very Heart
Of pain

And then
Dips
Us into
The infinity
Of peace
That
Sends us
Back Again
Into
The heart
Of pain . . . .

Yes, silence
Taught
Us much today . . . .
We learned
That love
Must have
Its way
And never count
The cost
We paid the cost
In silence
And in joy
While in the very
Heart of pain.

Somewhere I was sitting on the grass, picking daisies. I was pulling off the petals, saying, "He loves me, he loves me not." Suddenly, two people were at my side. They seemed to be transparent. You looked at them, and there they were. You looked again, and you could see through them—or, at least, so it seemed.

They were not picking daisies; they were talking both to themselves and to me. I was not thinking of anything "spiritual" at the moment. I was playing this game with God. I really knew that he loved me; still, the daisies were so sweet. I like to play games like this with God.

One was saying, "I am God's Solitude." The other was saying, "I am God's Silence." Solitude said that she was the friend of God, much more important than the Silence of God. And so they went on, arguing between themselves.

I said, "Don't you people know that the silence of God is quite different from solitude? You seem to have come from the place where God abides, yet you have not understood this. The silence of God is his love given to someone who walked to the silver sands, to the edge of the sea of infinity. Because he was drawn with his whole being to enter this sea, he did enter. This silence of God is nothing else than the complete following of Christ.

"This silence of God is pain beyond measure. Those who enter are plunged into God's knowledge, God's healing, and God's power. Have you forgotten that when he said, 'Love one another as I have loved you,' he made us heirs, children of the Father? At the same time, to those few who entered his silence, he gave his own knowledge, and the power to heal and to bring people to him. And have you forgotten that all these powers rest on the very slender thread of faith, on which silence rests also?

"Solitude usually walks with silence, but silence does not need solitude. Silence possesses solitude in itself. He who enters the depths of God's heart leaves solitude at its door, because the silence of God envelops him. Solitude is a way to silence. It can lead people to the silver sands, but it does not necessarily plunge them into the infinite sea of tremendous silence, pain, joy, crucifixion, and resurrection.

"Solitude prepares a person for silence, prepares him to approach the silver sands and jump into the waters of the sea. Then solitude leaves the silver sands and walks again the rocky pavements of city and country, calling, whispering, proclaiming God to anyone who will listen.

"Slowly, solitude gathers a small group that she will lead to the silver sands. Solitude will lead others into the busy marketplace. There they will serve the poor, the sick, the lonely, just as the Lord served us. Solitude will console. Solitude will enter families and bring peace where there is strife. Solitude has much work to do, and among these works is to bring a small group of people to the silver sands of the immense sea."

This is what I said to the two who were sitting at my side. Then they vanished.

The entrance into the silence of God is not a matter of thinking. It is an action. You stand on the silver sands and then move into that sea of infinity. You must plunge deeply into it. There is no bottom. Its depths will continue the rest of your life.

This sea can also turn into a mountain, for God can do all things. So, sometimes, in the great silence of God, you are not swimming but climbing, climbing slowly and painstakingly to the summit of the mountain, even though this summit is not visible. It isn't because it is covered with snow or anything else, though there is a kind of fog, a sweet and beautiful fog that you see sometimes in the early morning in the fall. That's how the summit appears, and you reach it only when you die.

In the immense silence of God, be it the sea of infinity or the mountain, you must go on because the incredible has been revealed to you: God's overwhelming love for you and for all mankind. You cannot resist this love. You continue onward, always onward. It may be in the depths of the sea or on the heights of the mountain, but you continue on. Love is a magnet that will not release you.

The only difficulty is that the deeper you go into the sea, or the higher you go up the mountain, the clearer are the desires, the hopes, and the dreams of mankind. You see them all before you. They are laid out like a map, with all its plains and contours and mountain ranges.

From the very beginning of the human race, men and women disobeyed God. However you wish to understand the story of Adam and Eve, one thing is certain: somewhere deep down in the heart of man is disobedience to God. Somewhere deep down in this same heart is the urge to kill. Cain killed his brother. Let that truth sink into our hearts, because this is what people have been doing since time immemorial—killing one another. Even today, in many parts of the world, what do you see? People killing each other. You see more. Killing is at least merciful. You see men torturing one another.

Over all this pain, touching the sky and rooted deeply in the silence of God, is a cross made out of wood. Think of what it means to hang on it. It was full of splinters, and flies crawled all over the wounds. The crown of thorns allowed no rest for the head.

Yes, God bleeds. Is that the result of an imagination running wild? I don't know. But I see that in each person who dies by the hand of his brother, in each person who is tortured by another, Christ bleeds. Christ is in eternal agony. There is no respite for him. War follows war. And the depths of the silence of God opens the eyes of my heart to behold what to me is like a vision.

I see the immense cross of Christ, which has its roots in the earth but touches the sky. I see that this cross is always in agony. As I turn my face away for just a minute to blot out the sight, I see a throne on the summit of the mountain. On the throne I see him who sat and talked to the Samaritan woman. I cry, because his pain has been my pain for so long. He answers me from the throne: "Catherine, until the end, until we meet, you will experience my pain. But then you will sit forever at my feet and experience my joy."

Hope is a gift of God. It appears when everything else is lost and when hopelessness seems to reign. The landscape that surrounds the silence of God is bleak. One stands in the middle of sheer cliffs that cannot be climbed, at least not by human effort.

From below, all I can do is look up at these immense cliffs, which seem to touch the sky. Of course, there is a distance between the cliffs and the sky, but because one is so deep down into the silence of God, the cliffs and the sky seem to touch. To climb these sheer cliffs seems utterly hopeless to the human mind.

But the human mind, having stood by the silver sands and jumped into the abyss of the infinite sea, is no longer merely human, and therefore hopeless. Hope must spring from somewhere, and it springs, as it usually does, from God. The cliffs are steep and slippery, and the deep silence of God hovers over you. These cliffs of hopelessness seem to grow taller.

This is the moment of trust. Can God provide you with

a ladder to climb to the top of these cliffs? Prayer doesn't seem possible. The Tempter assails you on all sides. Faith alone has hold of you, as if by a small hook and slender wire. But you have to do the impossible. You have to pick up that hook and wire, which are lying at your feet, and attach them to yourself. You hook them on to your ragged clothes. You begin to experience a new power—and Christ laughs.

Did you ever hear Christ laugh? He used to dance and clap his hands like all Jewish children. I don't know if he danced as an adult, but he must have danced when he was a youth. In the immense silence you can hear the clapping of his hands, and the laughter of God. Quicker than a streak of lightning, you feel a tug of tremendous power on this slender wire. Hope surges in your heart as you are carried up, up, back into the big wide world of sun and moon, of beautiful trees and lovely flowers. It is because this gives Christ such great delight that he laughs.

That's how it is. But, alas, people do not believe in God's power. One after another, they jump off bridges and take sleeping pills. I know, because I have experienced the same temptation. In my book *Fragments From My Life*,* I talk about these temptations. Water can look inviting and peaceful from the top of the Brooklyn Bridge. There were many, many times when I stood at the feet of sheer cliffs and couldn't see the hook and the wire to which I could attach myself. But it was always there—barely visible perhaps—but always there.

However, in the great silence of God, even when you cannot pray with your lips, because they are cold and you

*Ave Maria Press, 1979.

cannot pronounce the words, the words are pronounced by your heart. And the prayer always is, "Have mercy on me, Lord, for I am perishing—perishing because I don't seem to believe in you. My faith is weak; strengthen it."

Once you have gone through this experience, nothing, nothing in this world will ever cause it to happen again. It is finished. Even the experience of martyrdom, I don't think, would repeat it. Martyrs receive special graces from God.

And so, on this thin hook and wire you surface into the fresh air. You lie down peacefully in a garden. Suddenly, the Wind, which is part of God's silence, passes by and whispers to you, "That was one of the tests. God tested you and did not find you wanting."

✳ The Mysteries of Silence

The road got steeper and the stones got sharper. The clouds were hanging over the stony path so that you could barely see it. A storm was brewing. I moved slowly, as one heavily burdened, though the only thing I carried was a shepherd's crook to help me walk. Still, the feeling of being heavily burdened was with me.

I came across a group of people screaming, yelling, and gesticulating. Two or three men were dragging a half-naked woman to where Christ was standing. I was deeply engrossed in my silence and really didn't want anything to do with it. My silence seemed to be a warm protection against the storm that was coming.

The woman was crying. I tried to make a detour, but there always seemed to be somebody in my way. So I stopped. I heard her accused of adultery, a crime punishable by stoning according to the Jewish law. They were screaming at Christ too.

In an unusual gesture, he bent down and began writing something on the sand; he was absolutely silent. So was I—utterly silent. He continued writing, then suddenly he broke the silence by saying, "If any one of you is without sin, let him cast the first stone." Then he continued to write.

The quality of the silence changed. Kneeling on the

sharp stones, and as if a thousand flashes of lightning were exploding around me, I knew, with a knowledge no one could ever take from me, the *mercy of God.* One by one the men left her, and the woman was standing there all alone. Christ broke the silence once again: "Is there no one to condemn you?" "No one, Lord," she said. "Then neither will I condemn you. Go, but don't sin any more."

She left, but I remained. Christ ceased writing on the sand. Then he sat down on a large stone and looked at me. I looked at him. Breaking my silence, I said, "Lord, I have just witnessed the immense mercy of God. Will I die for having seen it?" For I was absolutely sure that no one could behold this outpouring of mercy that flashed like lightning and live.

The Lord shook his head and smiled and said, "No, Catherine. That is not what you are here for. You are here to become a silent witness to this mercy. Now that you have had it burnt into your soul, now that you know what mercy is, *go and be merciful.*"

The sharp stones disappeared. The little path was not there any more. There was a beautiful garden, and the olive trees were in bloom. There was a group of people marching, brandishing arms. No one seemed to oppose them. They were walking over a small knoll. Then they opened the gate of the garden and entered.

It was someone's property. They all stopped. Out of their midst came a man who was not armed in any way, and he walked straight towards Christ, who stood a short distance ahead of those who were with him. Then this man, putting his arms across Christ's shoulders with a sort of gentle hug, kissed him on both cheeks. It seemed at that moment that the earth stood still; there was not the slightest breath of wind anywhere. The silence of nature penetrated my heart like the silence of a funeral.

The armed crowd seemed to sense this also. They kept looking to the right and to the left, as if trying to locate where the silence was that enveloped everything.

I leaned against a tree. I was too weak to stand up without support. I was beholding the betrayal of God by man. It was not the betrayal of a nation by a nation. It was not the betrayal of one family member by another. Oh, no! It was the betrayal of God by man.

To my amazement, nothing happened. I was not close enough to see if Jesus returned the kiss. I simply know that Judas said, "This is the man."

After that there were bits of conversation that drifted past me in the great silence into which I entered. For I did enter a great silence. No one spoke. It was like a void, and I was in its midst. There was only one booming thought, which seemed to cover everything with death: God had been betrayed by man. And by a man who knew who he was. Betrayed by a man who had been with him for almost three years of his public life. Betrayed by a man who was his close companion. Yes, this was the only thought which penetrated the void of my silence.

The crowd passed me by as if I were not there. I walked on. On the occasions when Pilate, Herod, and the High Priest spoke to Christ, I seemed to be in a corner someplace, listening. But I couldn't hear anything. Nothing penetrated the void of silence in which I lived. The void itself was inflicting pain on me—pounding into my head like a crown of thorns the words, "*Man betrayed God; Man betrayed God!*"

Somehow I arrived at Golgotha, and there I stood before the cross and beheld God crucified. His head was slumped forward, the crown of thorns askew on his head, causing immense pain. I did not dare lift my eyes too often. Finally I stood up, and the strange void of silence began falling from me. I began to feel free of its terrible embrace.

It was then that I looked at Christ. It seemed as if I had grown taller, so that when he lifted his head and looked at me, our eyes were on the same level. I was going to say something, but his voice broke the silence first. And it was strong, even though coming from a crucified man.

He said, "Catherine, yesterday you witnessed the mercy of God. You saw Our mercy and you thought that was the whole of it. No, child, the mercy of God is infinite. I shall pray now to my Father." He cried out, "Father, forgive them, for they do not know what they are doing." And having said this, he looked at me. For a split second I thought I saw a smile on his face.

Then he went on: "Now, Catherine, you have seen the immensity, the infinity, of God's mercy. Go forth now and be merciful to everyone, but above all, *be merciful to your enemies.*"

Silence vanished for a few moments, then returned, enveloping me with a beggar's cloak. I looked at myself and saw that I was poorly dressed, very much as Russian pilgrims are. My skirts were long, catching hold of all kinds of prickly plants as I walked along. My dress seemed almost disgraceful, it was so beggarly, so poor. I did not have a needle or thread to make a seam, so it just dragged along the ground.

I had a black shawl, for it was cold. (Sometimes silence

is cold.) The shawl was clasped below my chin with a large thorn. Underneath the shawl I wore a multicolored blouse, something like Joseph's coat. It seemed that I had picked the blouse up someplace where someone had thrown it away. I had washed it and it was quite clean. Slowly I travelled over a path that led to a large city. Soon the path changed into a larger road; then it melted into innumerable streets. No one seemed to pay any attention to this old woman with a black shawl, a ragged cloak, and old slippers. But I was becoming tired.

Several streets came together at a kind of plaza, with park benches scattered around it. I sat down on one of these benches and soon became lost in the vast silence of God. I could only dimly hear the noise of the passing traffic. The silence of God is all-absorbing, and I was plunged into it.

Suddenly a beggar appeared from nowhere. His pants were ragged too, frayed at the ends. He had long hair, which shone a little, even though there was no sun. He wore a woolen tunic and had something on his shoulder. Perhaps it was a water gourd, for it was rather flat.

I looked at him and he looked at me. At first, that is all that happened. But he was bolder than I. Every time someone passed by this little plaza, he arose and put out his hand, asking for alms. It reminded me of the days of the Great Depression, when people were begging five cents for a cup of coffee.

He never said anything. He just extended his hand. Each time he received a coin, he placed it on the bench in a small pile and looked at it. One time when he was looking at it, big tears filled his eyes, falling on the pennies, nickels, and dimes. They were heavy, men's tears. The strangest thing happened. The coins on which his tears fell turned into something fantastically beautiful. Again, I was lost for a while in God's silence. It was as if I existed and did not exist at the same time. It was as if the whole world became mine, but it only lasted a few seconds.

I became aware of the beggar again. He turned his face towards me and I looked into his eyes. I had often read of the Transfiguration of Jesus on Mount Tabor, and something of this happened that day on that bench in that plaza. The beggar was transformed. He himself shone with a light that I could not endure, and his small pile of coins was transfigured as well. As in previous times, a voice came to me as if out of a wind. It said:

"Catherine, this money, whether given out of abundance or out of scarcity, like the coins of the widow in the temple, is blessed. And those who gave it are blessed. But those who passed by and did not see you or me will not come to know my Father unless they repent. Understand another mystery of the Trinity. I am teaching you as children are taught in the first grade. My mysteries are not found in theology books. No, my mysteries are found in loving me. Those who love me, and especially those who have come to the silver sands and plunged into the sea of my infinity, they are the ones who learn the mysteries of the Trinity.

"It is time for you to learn them too. You know a little about the mystery of God's mercy. Now you have to learn about the consolation of God. Yes, I became man, and like all other men, I sought, when I was on the earth, consolation. I received very little of it, and so did you. But right now, see the little pennies and coins that people have given me. These are my consolation because they who gave loved me. This, in truth, is the consolation of the Trinity.

"Enter into this mystery, and understand that you console the Trinity through me. As you console me, you console my Father and the Holy Spirit, and my mother as well. So, do not forget: I was a man, and I sought consolation, and I did not receive very much. Nor will you if you are following my footsteps into my immense silence. My silence is the silence of people who desire to console their God."

Before I could say a word—I was awestruck by the transformation of this poor man—he was gone. But the little pile of money was still there. Out of the wind again came his voice, "Take this money and give it to those who need it. It is blessed." Then I was enveloped by the silence again.

I sat a long time on that bench, and many poor people came to sit beside me. To each one I gave part of this holy money, though they did not know it was holy. For a long time I entered into what I thought was the total silence of God. Of course it was not total. In our relationship with God there is always "more." But at that time it seemed to me that I was touching the furthest depths of the silence of God.

Towards evening, a policeman came and said to me, "Woman, you have been sitting here all day. Move on now." I said, "Can't I sit here all night too?" He replied, "Well, yes, if you want to. But you haven't eaten all day. I have some sandwiches my wife gave me. Here, take some." Then he left.

I seemed to be lost, but not in the consolation of God. I was lost in the consolation of man. I seemed to be surrounded by a crowd of silent people, poor people. They were pressing in on me. My heart was open to everyone, for those who enter the great silence of God lose the key to their own hearts. Anyone can knock and walk in. But this was the world—the whole world—coming at me.

I asked myself, "Who are all these people?" Suddenly I understood. I was looking at wounded people. I realized that the whole world was wounded in one way or another. The rich were wounded by their riches, and the poor by their poverty. Everyone, without exception, was wounded.

It was night. There were no stars. Still the people thronged silently around me. This time it was not Christ who was begging; it was these people. They each extended both of their hands towards me, and with a whisper that was like a rhythmic song, they begged me to cure their wounds. They were saying that they could not continue to live with them. It was a most frightening thing! An innumerable crowd all whispering to be helped and extending their hands. I do not know anything about curing. I can't cure anything, let alone people. I could pray for them, but curing, no. That was not my gift in the silence of God.

So, I started praying for them. I prayed the prayer Jesus taught us: "Our Father, who art in heaven, hallowed be thy Name...." The whispering changed. The hands were still outstretched, but slowly everyone began repeating the prayer. I realized quickly that not everyone had known the prayer. There were Muslims, Jews, all kinds of people in the crowd.

I said, "Lord, what shall I do with all these wounded people? I cannot understand why *everyone* is wounded.

No one seems to have escaped the deep spiritual wounds inflicted on them by the world. What is it? What must I do?"

It seemed that I was being pushed against a wall by all these people, and there was no place to go. They continued to clamor in many languages and in a variety of ways. My heart was filled with prayer for them. I cried to God to come to my help. I recited the psalm, "Out of the depths I have cried to you, O Lord." Help me! You promised you would!

I thought of the Good Samaritan. But he had only one person to help. Here there were millions of people, each crying out to God for help and comfort. And while they were crying out, Satan was walking proudly around. He had a smile on his lips. He knew that these wounds were capable of leading people down the road to perdition.

I thought, too, of Job, and of how difficult it was to heal his spiritual and physical wounds.

Suddenly, I heard a voice, the strongest voice I have ever heard. There was a field of poppies close by, and a man clothed in white sitting among the poppies. The wind picked up his voice and brought it to me as on previous occasions. I heard him say, "Blessed are the poor. . . ." When he finished the beatitudes there was a deeper calm and joy among the people.

But they still seemed to need something else to salve their wounds, some balm that was not present in the words of the beatitudes. Majestically, the man in white stood up, and he was revealed as Jesus Christ. Many of the people still did not know who he was.

He told his apostles to lay out fish and bread. Then he fed the millions who surrounded me. After he had fin-

ished feeding them, many hundreds of baskets of left-
overs were taken away by the people. The people were
more consoled by the food. But there still remained
something that was not completely healed.

Next, I saw another table being laid out. I saw the
apostles loading these tables with huge quantities of
bread and wine. "Oh," I said to myself, "now he is *really*
going to feed them." And so he did. He fed all those millions with his own Body and Blood. There was no distinc-
tion here between Jew and Muslim and Gentile. He fed
those who knew who he was and those who didn't, fed
them with this food of eternal life. He died for all peoples, so he fed all peoples, and healed all.

The people vanished. I looked at him once more. He
said to me, "Catherine, this is another mystery of God
which you must learn. I love all mankind. I have reconciled all mankind to myself. This is why I came into the
world, to be crucified and to reconcile all mankind to my
Father. Go forth and spread this Good News to
everyone."

✳ The Mystery of the Church

The entire scene changed. I was in a large room. Actually, it was more like a cathedral, like Hagia Sophia in Constantinople, which I had seen once. A large number of priests were assembled. There were priests from every century, from the earliest days of Christianity until the present.

They were talking to one another; some were arguing. Some seemed about to come to blows! They were defending something. It reminded me of some of the councils of the Church, in which, I had read, there were fierce arguments. I began to chuckle a bit at the absurdity of it, but then I started to cry. A sense of fear surrounded me like a womb. Just as a child is enclosed in its mother's womb, so this sense of fear enveloped me. The number of priests present seemed too large for the room, and the room seemed to grow larger to accommodate them.

I seemed to be perched on top of a colonnade so that I could look down and witness all this. What I saw brought both joy and a terrible sorrow into my heart. The crowd of priests suddenly parted, and through the aisle thus formed came a procession of light-filled people in two long columns. I realized that they were all saints. Tremendous light poured from them, and this light sought to penetrate the hearts of the priests. It entered those with open hearts, but others it could not.

At the very head, and in the center of the two columns, walked Mary, the Queen of all Saints. She is the Queen of all the canonized and uncanonized saints, represented by the two columns.

I recognized some of the faces—St. Augustine, St. Francis of Assisi, St. John of the Cross, St. John Vianney, and others. When I saw them reach the altar, a great joy overcame me. It was as if God said to me, "You see, I have saints, people who have followed me to the very end." St. Stephen came into view. I heard his beautiful words, "Lord, do not hold this sin against them."

There were also, in both columns, thousands of martyrs, who had passed through the fire of blood. A great hymn arose. It did not break the silence of God, but it was a heavenly music of a kind I had never heard before. Overwhelmed by his silence, which enveloped this music, I fell prostrate before the Lord, whom I did not see but of whose presence I was aware.

The music continued, and my joy grew greater and greater. My joy blended with the very joy of God. This is part of the mystery of the silence of God. It is really sobornost, man's union with God. Man begins to feel a little of what God feels—his joy and sorrow. It seemed that my heart would break, so heavenly was the music.

The procession continued. We make distinctions between "beatified" saints and "canonized" saints. However man imagines these distinctions, it does not work that way with God. A saint is a saint! In one column, as I mentioned, were saints canonized by God long before official canonization by the Church. There were Mary Magdalen, and St. Peter, who was called "the Rock" by the Lord, and upon whom he built his Church.

There was Zacchaeus, too, and many others.

The music now was a music of gladness. It was the song of people who are forgiven, of people who are reconciled with Christ, of people who realize that they are sinners but are created in the image and likeness of God. They had followed Christ and his word in their own humble and hidden ways. In this procession were the myriads of women down through the ages who had tended the sick, fed the poor, and taken from their own mouths bread to feed these poor. No doubt many of these people you would have recognized. Saints live among us all the time!

What a beautiful sight it was, and the music was indeed exquisite. But suddenly a sour note entered the room. The people of God, the Church, which had been freed from the law of the Old Testament, freed from many laws that had little or nothing to do with God or the beatitudes, suddenly seemed infested with little worms. Then the worms turned into snakes that began to slither across the marble floor. Only the saints saw them. The others were too preoccupied with their own ideas to notice them.

I, from my vantage point on top of the colonnade, began to see unusual sights.

I saw St. Thomas Aquinas step out from the line of saints and ask his superior about burning his theological works. He said he had seen God as he was praying before his crucifix. From that moment on he considered his writings as straw. I asked myself, "How did St. Thomas learn the mystery of God?" He had written so profoundly about the mysteries of the faith.

The answer came to me as if spoken by Christ: "The way to know me is not through books, but to pray and do what the woman with the issue of blood did. She pulled at my garment so that I would turn around and notice her. Catherine, this does not mean that you should put aside the gifts which I have given to you and to others— gifts of intellect and the like. No. You must use all my gifts all the time. My Father has given them to you and to humanity so that humanity might progress towards a peaceful life on earth.

"But the way to learn about my mysteries is to be very silent, very quiet, and to wait. Then, one day I shall come and reveal my mysteries to those who awaited my coming."

For a short period it seemed that I was deaf and dumb, that I had lost all hearing and sight. Listening to the words of the Lord does that to me. Slowly my senses returned. I kept peering down on the scene below. Now I understood why the superior of St. Thomas would not allow him to burn his writings: generations would have been bereft of the many profound and beautiful things he wrote.

Pope John XXIII appeared. From my colonnade I could hear him ordering people to open some windows! He was having a hard time. I wondered why they were trying to open windows. Then, below me, in the aisle, I saw Bishop Jansen. He looked very ascetical. He was preaching and attracting to himself a great crowd of followers.

He was preaching mainly that we are great sinners, and

that therefore there must be long preparations for the reception of Holy Communion. There were many other restrictive rules in his preaching. I shook my head. I asked myself what would happen when all the windows were opened. There would be a tremendous upheaval in the Church. I realized that this upheaval was overdue for the people of God. The Church had acquired many "Jansenistic" habits, which had continued into the present day.

The reasons for the "open windows" became clearer. In the sixteenth century there had been a great disruption in the Body of Christ, his Church. Many small sects had sprung up since then. And even before this disruption there was a break between the Eastern and Western Churches. In this latter part of the twentieth century a renewed cry arose from the hearts of men for unity with one another. It appeared to me that this could happen, but that some catastrophe might have to take place before men began to fall on their knees, hold hands across the whole world, and once again have a common faith in God.

I seemed to fall asleep at this point. In my dreams I was lifted up into some kind of heaven. Then I began to understand that God blots out our intellectual understanding in order to bring forth from our souls a deeper spiritual understanding. I understood that whatever catastrophe humanity might have to face, it would be beneficial in the long run, a means of bringing men and women to God. Then all would cry out together, "Lord, out of the depths I cry to you. Please take me out of this and bring me back to where you desire. Give me understanding so that I can cherish the earth as well as my brother. We must all be one, one with each other and one with you."

I awoke, and this time my eyes focused on the priests themselves. I looked at them with new eyes, touched by God. I saw that there were many holy priests. Nevertheless, I wanted to change seminaries and infuse them with the law of love. I heard the words of Christ in my ears: "A new commandment I give you, that you love one another."

Because I love priests more than any other people in the world after God and Our Lady, I cried to heaven, "Abba, Father, open their ears. Bless their minds that they may understand that they are *shepherds* and nothing else. Help them become poor, giving away whatever they don't need. May they live in simpler dwellings and not rich presbyteries. Help them, Father, to teach people how to love so that your children do not run after cults of all kinds. Lord, give them your blessing. Father, wake them up! Lord Jesus, they are your brothers and heirs of the kingdom. Send your Spirit to enlighten them. Why are they not on the highways and byways like St. Francis, preaching your gospel? Father, what has happened to the leaders of your Church?"

There I was, sitting on that colonnade in a huge cathedral. The voice of Christ came to me again: "Catherine, love my priests. They are so dear to me. I pour out my heart to them, but so many block their hearts against me. Pray for priests. Beseech my Father to cure them, for they are sick with self-centeredness and self-satisfaction. They are sick with loneliness, rejection, and fear. Pray that they may be like St. Stephen and St. Sebastian. Pray that they may not be afraid to be martyrs, which means to give birth to thousands in the faith. And above all, pray that they stay within the Church. The laity today still receive their birth from the womb of the Church. It is there that they receive the gifts of faith, of love, and of hope. The question is, what do they, and the priests whom I have called especially to follow me, do with these gifts I give them? So pray for priests."

Again I found myself in completely new surroundings. The Lord had picked me up by the hair and transported me to another place. I did not understand this spiritual traveling, which evidently was part of the great silence of God. However, I knew that once you had entered it, all you could do was follow him, no matter where he led. True, you heard many things, but that did not mean that you were not silent. What you saw and what you heard passed before you like a series of pictures painted by God himself, but the silence was never broken.

This time I truly did not know where I was. From out of the mountains, boulders, and paths there came a sense of fear. I became utterly silent in my heart and soul. It was a peculiar type of silence. It was not the silence of peace, but the silence of pain, of strife, of unpeace. I wondered about this.

Then, slowly, my silence was filled with people. As I looked closely, I saw that they were nuns. Once again, a procession was being formed, another procession of both canonized and "unofficially canonized" saints—all beloved of God. Gazing at the uncanonized ones, I had a flashback in my mind to a sermon I heard once that impressed me immensely.

A priest preaching in France once said to his congregation, "I am going to ask you a question. Think about it and give me an answer in writing if you wish, or speak openly next Sunday. I have just returned from Constantinople. I saw there the heroism of the Russian women. There was very little work available. I watched for a whole week. I saw some of the married women, in order to obtain a few pennies for their families, become prostitutes. At the end of the week I prostrated myself before the Lord and asked him this question, 'Were they saints or sinners?' What do you think, were they saints or sinners?" I never forgot that sermon.

This insight often came to me in the immense silence of God—how many uncanonized saints we have in the world. There are many who lead very tragic lives, but holy ones. I knew a woman who lived on seven dollars a week. She had very little to eat, and most of the food she gave to her infant son. I believe there are many such people in the world.

The sky became dark, as it often does in the silence of God. Lightning and thunder seemed to surround me. I hadn't said a word. As I said, pictures, as if painted by God, passed before me, supernatural in quality, as might be expected in the silence of God.

I said to myself, "That was an interesting question posed by the priest, but why am I seeing pictures of nuns?" I closed my eyes; I was tired, not of the silence of God but of the pictures he was constantly bringing into the silence. Suddenly I realized that the thunder and the lightning was coming from the hearts of the nuns!

They were filled with unrest. The majority seemed to be discussing modes of dress. They were very interested in their attire, interested in discarding any form of dress that set them apart as nuns. They fought against this distinctiveness with their hearts and souls. It was a very tragic thing to see. The deeper one penetrates into the silence of God, the deeper one sees into the tragedy of a soul fighting with itself. A great fear comes upon you, because the struggle with oneself is also the struggle with the powers of darkness.

Deeper and deeper I entered into the silence of God. What can I say? I am a nothing and a nobody. I have never been a nun. I was acquainted with them as a child in school, but I knew nothing of their interior life. But I believed that in this instance of the clothing, they were in defiance of God. The Holy Father had told them to dress otherwise. When the Vicar of Christ speaks, obedience is the only answer.

I noticed that there was little obedience, and not only in this matter of clothing. A strange rebellion seemed to imprison them. One even stood up and challenged the Holy Father! I do not know what she said. I was lost in the silence, a sad silence. It was filled with tears.

But my tears do not amount to anything. Or do they? Why shouldn't an old woman weep over a group of women who have forgotten that they were called by God to become his spouses, his lovers, his servants, his followers? Yes, all I could do was cry, and cry I did.

The Russians say that tears can wash away the sins of others. I fervently hope this is so. For all I can do for nuns, whom I really love with a great love, is cry, even though they may not understand or know about it. In this great silence of God I truly understood what it is to love another. The words of Christ, "Love one another," were now a reality in my soul. These nuns were my sisters, and I prayed for them ceaselessly.

My surroundings changed again. I was alone, totally alone, except for a fear that entered my heart and would not leave. I looked around. The scenery was rather flat. Here and there some high knolls reared their heads. There were some lakes and rivers—all polluted. The fields smelled of some chemical sprayed by an airplane.

I did not like the place. I wanted to leave, and yet I wanted to remain in the great silence of God. When one is in the great silence of God, places do not really matter. You are speaking intimately with God. The entry deep into this silence eventually results in a mysterious speech with him. This has to be experienced to be understood. It is a form of sobornost in which man is united with God by the thin but strong thread of silence.

As I said, I did not like the place. The silence captivated me, but the surroundings did not. Quite suddenly, the wind came. It lifted me up and placed me in a large city. From there I made a pilgrimage across the land, traveling thousands of miles and visiting hundreds of cities. All this happened in a flash.

I was no longer meeting priests and nuns. I found myself immersed in the everydayness of the laity. It was extraordinary. Now I was with families, now I was talking to married couples, now I was surrounded by youth, now the aged crowded around me. At one point I found myself walking along assembly lines, and then speaking to the "jet set" along Park Avenue.

Memories came back to me. I recalled the time I was invited to Park Avenue to give a talk to about forty women. It was in a home. They did not wish to go to a lecture hall, as it might have been unsanitary. I gave the talk, and when I finished, the butler stood holding my coat, which had come from a Harlem clothing room. It had an obvious rip in it, and the butler held it disdainfully.

One of the ladies said that she would give me another coat, but I declined, and asked for a taxi to return to Harlem. She said, "Oh no, my car will take you." This was one of the few times I rode in a Rolls Royce. The silence of God in that car was an angry silence. Later, they sent me a coat to replace my torn coat. We would often pawn it and then reclaim it.

Pope Pius XI had fostered the idea of the laity participating in the mission of the Church with the hierarchy. The encyclicals of these early days clarified the road I had to travel. I dreamed of engaging in some kind of action which would help the Church. What exactly it would be was hidden from me in the silence of God.

There came a day, however, when all these things were revealed to me. It happened as I was travelling rapidly across the many cities and towns and villages of the world, preaching the gospel. The mystery of darkness was revealed to me. I witnessed greed and avarice, the sins of the Old Testament to which I seldom paid any attention. Mea culpa!

Avarice differs from greed inasmuch as avarice hoards everything for itself and keeps everything for itself. Greed simply desires to possess money, power, and prestige. It doesn't care if such things pass out of its possession for a while, as long as they are always available. Avarice and greed are handmaidens to pride. Arrogance and pride rule over them, and they do the bidding of pride.

Now, in the silence of God, while I crossed the land and listened to others preach the gospel, I found very few who *really* preached it. Oh, there were holy people among the laity who had given up everything and followed Christ, but they were few and far between. There were still so many who did not believe in Christianity—the Hindus, the Moslems, the Brahmins, and so forth. These all crowded around me and I realized that many of them were more Christian than the majority of Christians.

I was tired. To traverse the world the way I was doing seemed to take centuries. Now I found the Holy Spirit asking me to rest and to pray about all I had seen, especially the Christians. I was only too glad to comply. I do not really know how to express it. After having seen everything that I saw, I began to cry. Tears came in the silence of God, and they filled the earth. A small body of water appeared, which gradually grew into a river. And this river of my tears went straight through the world. What good it did I do not know, but I could not stop crying. That was my first reaction when the Holy Spirit told me to be quiet and pray about what I had seen.

One cannot analyze these things, only experience them, and that only in a small way. Do not imagine that there was any tremendous vision. There was simply an attempt to follow Christ. I knew that Christ had also cried. Perhaps this crying was a deeper entry into his silence.

I continued to think about what I had seen. Though there were tears on my face, the Tempter came. It seemed that I was in his hands. He presented to me a very "logical" argument.

"Now, Catherine," he said, "you have seen the hopelessness of the Christian Church, especially the Catholic Church. You see that its adherents, the laity, are not really interested in anything except making money. They are interested in the immediate satisfaction of their desires.

Then, the moment they acquire this satisfaction, they become more frustrated. Look at the sexual immorality, the daily business 'rip-offs.' Everybody does it! It is time you yourself forgot all this silence of God nonsense and started living—really living!—in the time you have left in your life. Live quietly and in peace. You have enough to be comfortable, so use it. Use it for yourself."

It was as if an evil wind were all around me. Trees bent and broke in the force of it. I was shaken like a reed in that wind, and all the time the whisper of the Tempter was in my ears:

"Why spend so many years in trying to bring the gospel of Christ to people who never listen? It all goes in one ear and out the other. Look at their actions. Those are the proof of the uselessness of it all."

The storm and the wind were frightful. What he was saying was partly true. I said to myself, "How is it possible for the Tempter to be truthful?" Then I awoke and I invoked the name of Mary. I made the sign of the cross and the wind subsided. Like a weary traveler, I went to sleep.

When I awoke, there was the Lord. He said, "You have been tempted because I need tempered steel to deal with the laity. They remember me, yet they forget me. Where the fault lies for their forgetting I am not ready to discuss. I simply say they have forgotten me. It is your business and others' to go forth, confronting them face to face, for that is the only way of bringing them to me. For when you are face to face with them, you love them, and once you love them, then I can speak through you."

Again, I found myself in different terrain. I was lifted up and suddenly surrounded with gentle mountains and beautiful trees. From this vantage point I saw the Church. It is not "churches" that arise out of the silence of God but *the Church*. There she stood, above the tree line, shining in the rays of the noonday sun. She was beautiful and simple, with her doors wide open, and into her streamed the rich and poor alike. I beheld the *Church*, and awe took hold of me. The words of the Old Testament came to me, "Take off your shoes; the place is holy."

Suddenly, a fire began to rage around her. Indeed, the place was holy and so was this fire. It was the fire of which Christ had spoken: "I have come to cast fire upon the earth, and what do I will but that it be enkindled." I looked into the fire and saw a Roman soldier pierce Christ's side with a lance. From his body came forth blood and water. At that moment I knew whence the Church had been born.

It was a beautiful building. The walls were transparent, as were the doors and the dome. All kinds of people walked through the doors in great simplicity and joy of heart. Then I heard a great sound, the united voice of the people of God. I knew beyond all doubt that this people was joined to Christ; he was their head and they were his members. A deep sense of adoration flowed from this people into the silence of God. It was so overwhelming that I could hardly bear it.

I looked again and the scene changed. A disruption, a dismemberment, a tearing apart seemed to be taking place. The doors through which so many people had passed were being barred. I shook my head and tried to clear my eyes, for they were filling up with tears. I said to myself, "It can't be happening that the people of God

are causing all this turmoil." But that was what was happening. They were tearing each other apart in my sight.
Each had his own idea of the Church. The "intellec-
tuals," who were supposed to be supporting the Church,
were arguing. Some were even denying the existence of
God. I know how they felt. I recalled standing in my little
room in Harlem, lifting my arms to God in anger. I cried
out, "Why are you allowing them to do these things to
the Negro? Look at their faces! Slavery still exists, only
in a different form. How is it that you allow things like
this?"

Then I slumped to the floor as if someone had hit me
over the head with a board. But I got up again, and lifted
my arms to God, this time crying out for the Indian.
Then I cried out for all those who had come to Canada
and the United States as immigrants like me. I prayed for
all those who were called "Dirty Polack," "Kike," "Bo-
hunk," "Dago," "Limey," "Frog." These epithets buzzed
around in my head like bees. I remembered trying to get a
job as a waitress in Toronto and the boss asking, "What
is your religion?" When I replied that I was a Catholic he
said, "We don't take Catholics here." As my father had
taught, I lifted the two arms of prayer and fasting, but
nothing seemed to help. That is when my two arms became the arms of justice.

I couldn't take it anymore. I had to speak out for inter-
racial justice, and for justice for other ethnic groups. I
became a pilgrim, ascending lecture platform after lecture platform, especially in Catholic colleges. I remember a moment of great joy when the Benedictines of Col-
legeville, Minnesota, accepted the first Negro student, as
did the Benedictine Sisters. I never forgot this. My grati-

tude was expressed in a constant prayer. But these occasions were so rare.

I looked at the Church again. There she was, beautiful, shining. I realized that she was the Bride of Christ. He had said that the gates of hell would not prevail against her. I knew that she was his beloved, and that he was all tenderness, all love, towards her. She passed in front of my eyes, emerging out of the deep silence into which I had been thrust.

I saw what the Church really was—the beloved of God. Not only was she his beloved but she served the people whom he loved, the poor. The people whom he had fed with loaves and fishes she now fed with bread and wine. From my soul rose an immense cry of adoration.

At the same time I saw what some Catholics were doing to their Church. I saw Catholics upset with sermons and homilies because not every priest could speak well. True, some priests stutter, some speak poorly, but people do not know the hidden glory of these priests.

I have been in a thousand churches and have listened to sermons by great preachers and unknown preachers. In a little church hidden in the woods I once heard the stuttering sermon of a priest who could barely put his sentences together. From the depth of the silence of God in which I was encased, I suddenly heard that sermon with new ears. It filled my heart with an immense joy. For out of the great silence of God I knew with a knowledge that nothing can obscure that when a priest preaches, God preaches. If the priest, though, considers that his sermons are lovely and profound, it is then that God turns his face away from him.

Yes, I saw the Church torn apart. I was going to weep, but then I saw Christ putting it back together again. And there was music in the air, filling her who had come from his side, and making her whole again.

Yes, I saw the Church. I do not know whence she came or how. But she was right there, beautiful, shining, with the rich and poor streaming into her. So I was at peace for a little while, because I knew that the Church is forever being restored and renewed in her Lord. We celebrate his resurrection once a year, but he restores his Church every moment of the day and night.

I relaxed among the pines. It was night. But brighter than all the stars and the moon was the Church, shining in the darkness. I heard a voice say, "Once more, Catherine, you are tasting of my immense silence. I want you to see the mystery of the Church. People may tear it apart, but I put it back together again. Have faith in my power. Your faith may seem to hang by a very thin string, but I will strengthen that slender string because you have to defend my Church."

* The Multicolored Vocation of Silence

I was in a forest and it was dark. The background was Russian—birches and tall fir trees. There were also the plain little fields that I loved so much when I was young. They were all filled with flowers. There were chipmunks there, and all kinds of little creatures that are not at all afraid of you. It brought back memories of my youth.

Suddenly it became darker. The memories of youth vanished. I could no longer see the birches, nor the fields. Towering above me were the tall pines that make a rushing noise when the wind comes to caress them.

I was then transported to different places in Russia. I was taken to all kinds of monasteries, and found myself talking with all kinds of monks. I asked each of them, "How do you survive molchanie?" They smiled and said, "The hardest thing to survive is not molchanie but the speech of other people!" I came to understand that for these desert people (outside of the cities, Russia is quite a desert) speech was difficult, but they engaged in it because they understood their vocation to be "multicolored." "What do you mean 'multicolored'?" I asked. One of them answered, "It means that our vocation to silence has many aspects to it."

"What do you mean exactly?" I insisted. "I am trying to understand molchanie, the great silence of God."

He said, "Remember when you yourself came to me years ago to receive a blessing? You and your husband were the first to come. That is the day I began to preach the gospel."

Yes, I remembered that day in Russia many years ago. My husband and I had paid a visit to a holy hermit. We heard afterward of the marvels of his speech. The peasants used to say, "It's as if Jesus Christ speaks when he speaks."

But I still wanted to know what "multicolored" meant. So I went to see St. Sergius, who is my favorite Russian saint. I said to him, "St. Sergius, can you tell me what the multicolored vocation to silence is all about?"

He smiled in his long beard and said, "Oh, yes, it is very simple. It means that one is totally at the disposition of God. It is the vocation of total abandonment to God. His call then takes on different colors.

"Sometimes you are called into the depths of his pain. Then it becomes dark, because pain has a dark color. It may be in Gethsemane, or before Pilate. His pain is very deep, and only a few are called to enter into it. But not only monks. Oh, no! Lay people as well are called. His deepest pain on the cross was his rejection by those he had helped, forgiven, and cured of their wounds. But this pain has to be experienced before one can experience the joy of Easter.

"Joy is another color—white, golden white. You become bathed by it and it seems as if your heart will burst in anticipation of your own resurrection. But there are other colors in the multicolored vocation of molchanie. Why don't you go to the other monks, St. Seraphim of Sarov, for example, and ask about the multicolored vocation? It is only in God's silence that you can understand it."

So I went to St. Seraphim of Sarov and asked him about the multicolored vocation. He said, "You already know about the darkness of pain and the whiteness of joy. There is also the color of gray. It is the vocation of eating with the poor, the good-for-nothings, and annoying the big shots and the rich. The vocation of grayness is living the gospel in the midst of closed hearts, in the midst of people who do not understand the very essence of the gospel. Grayness is knocking at doors that never open. It is hurling stones against walls that never fall down. Grayness is the vocation of trying to enter men's hearts, which are like stone. Stones are gray, Catherine; stones are gray. We must embrace this gray vocation as we come out of the silence of God. It is a tragedy beyond explanation.

"Now, clothed with these colors, you become a spiritual father or mother. You have a vocation to be in the silence of God, yet speak. You remain in the silence of God, yet the latch on the door of your heart is never closed. Somebody may come and ask you to be his or her spiritual father or mother. Because this is your vocation, you accept. At one and the same time you are in the silence of God and speaking. Spiritual paternity or maternity is in itself a multicolored vocation."

I traveled in my imagination to another monastery and asked the same question about the multicolored vocation. The abbot blessed me and said, "Come with me." He brought me to the chapel and left me alone. He said, "Now ask *him* what the multicolored vocation is."

I asked God. He smiled and said, "Well, little by little I will tell you all about it. But it *is* multicolored, and it will take you a little while to understand the mystery of each color. By and by I will reveal all the colors to you."

A Pilgrim of Silence and Pain

What is my answer? Listen!
There is no use . . .
I cannot hide,
I am a pilgrim of silence and pain.

You walked barefoot
On the dusty roads of Palestine,
The Palestine that was so small.
I, your pilgrim, travel on ships
        and planes.
On roads and streets, across the
        sea, the air, the land,
To which Your Palestine would
        be a little nook,
A square,
A tiny part of my immense
        kaleidoscopic whole.
                And yet Your footprints are
                everywhere.

And I
I walk in them.
My steps are slow
For I am wounded too,
Even as You . . .
By You, my love . . . for You,
And them.
The wounds drip, drop by drop
On ship, on land, and in the air.
My blood—or is it Your Blood in
    me?—falls everywhere.

Gone are the days of speech . . .
Of just and flaming anger,
Of words like swords in Your
    defense.
Today I speak in silence
And through my wounds—or are
    they Yours?—
Alone among the noisy crowds,
I am a pilgrim of silence and of pain.
And everywhere I leave a gift,
A drop or two of blood,
Not knowing anymore if it is
    mine or Yours.

I am a pilgrim seeking You
Yet giving You to all.
For it is You, my Lord
Who meets me in each one I see,
        or touch or pass.
How strange and how incredible.
A mystery so profound
And I so small and foolish!

I lose You in so many, Lord
For they will not welcome You
        into their homes
And I run again, with wounds
        that bleed,
With wounds that gape
A little more with every step,
But I run on and on
For I must find You, and at the
        same time, I must give You
To all I see and meet and touch.

Yes, I must find You,
And give You to all
Through *Silence*
and through
Pain.
ALLELUIA!

The silent monks of Russia were not the only people I
had to visit. The tall pines and the birch trees opened up,
and all the deserts of the world began to flow past me as if
they were one vast river. Sand, trees, vegetation—every-

thing blended into one. The snows of the north seemed to flow into the deserts of the south. Hindu holy men appeared. Then I saw high mountains, where the Tibetan wise men lived. I was transported to the Amazon and saw native medicine men, also standing at the edge of the silver sands.

I was on a pilgrimage. It seemed as if God wanted me to see all the silent ones of the earth. He touched my shoulder and said, "Go and discover the many faces of my silence, which flows from my Heart, the Heart of the most Holy Trinity, and encompasses the whole universe. Most people do not know of this silence because they do not take the time to enter into it. Go!"

I trudged mile after mile and talked to so many silent ones that I lost count. All of these people were ordinary, not big shots or important. They were little people. One or two out of each community received the call to enter God's infinite silence. And I followed them. I plunged into the silence and into the heart of each person.

These people were lost in the silence of God. It was as if the Lord had taken them beyond all boundaries and placed them in a land where all lands meet. They were still on the earth, and yet it seemed they had left the earth. They were on their way to the parousia. When you approached them they didn't speak, but you knew that they were on the edge of the parousia. Everything around them breathed the peace that reigns there.

These people were so utterly immersed in the silence of God that you could almost touch it. It was like a shimmering, cascading light that emanated from each of them, of which they seemed to be oblivious. In the presence of these people immersed in the silence of God, you clearly realize what violence is. In the presence of such silence, the nature of violence is exposed. You can almost see violence stalking about in the night, trying in some way to stamp out the silent ones.

I continued my travels across the world. I did see violence conquer some of these silent ones. In a word, I saw martyrs. I saw some of these silent ones bedecked in glory. Their bodies were tortured; they were dragged around on the ground. Everywhere, the silent ones of God allowed themselves to be violated by violence. In place of clothes they were all covered with a bloody mantle. Yes, many of the silent ones across the world were becoming martyrs, and strangely enough, my heart rejoiced.

I didn't feel pity or any of those feelings you are supposed to feel when you see those who are totally lost in the silence of God become martyrs. I rejoiced because martyrdom is the cradle of faith.

Yes, an infinite joy overcame me, and I began to sing in a loud voice. Suddenly, right next to me, I heard the voice of the Lord. He said, "Catherine, keep on singing. Martyrdom is the greatest gift I can give to man, and the greatest gift man can give to me. So sing, because you don't know who of Madonna House is going to be martyred tomorrow. Maybe it will be you."

Silence is like a desert. It has ripples in the sand that look like waves. Seen from the back of a camel, these sandy waves seem eternally trying to catch up with the waves which have gone before. If you walk through the sands it is often knee-deep. The temperature can rise to 150 degrees in the daytime, and down to 40 degrees at night. To really see the moon and the stars you have to go to the desert.

The desert is beautiful, but for some reason you cannot pay attention to it. Maybe it is the starkness of the desert, but what confronts you contantly is the desire for martyrdom. This desire grows in the hearts of all those who have stood on the shore of the silver sands and plunged into the immense sea of God's infinity.

Now I ask you quite simply: Who wants to be a martyr? Who wants to accept it, even for the sake of the Beloved, even for the sake of Jesus Christ? And yet, there *are* people who look for it, pray for it, hope for it, welcome it.

Consider the martyrs in the Roman coliseum. Who can count them all? Some we know, and they have been canonized, but they should all be canonized, for they all died for Christ. Many not only forgave but, like St. Stephen, implored the Lord not to hold against them what their persecutors were doing.

It is not easy to explain this desire for martyrdom. You must enter a whole new dimension, cross the bridge of God's silence into his love. It is because you are completely in love with him that your desire for identification with the Martyred Beloved reaches such incredible proportions. You stagger through the sands like a person intoxicated with love, seeking your Lover and willing to hold onto him in whatever way you can.

Back and forth, back and forth he walks the desert of your soul crying out, "Don't you know how much I love you!" You answer, "You are God. You understand. You brought me to your silence, and your silence brought me to your love. And now I want to identify myself with you completely. I want to die for you."

Up and down, up and down, you walk in the desert.

Your footprints become deeply imbedded in the sand. You continue walking, seeking for that door. It isn't to everyone that the door from silence into martyrdom is opened. Martyrdom is the full flowering of silence.

When the Indians tortured Jean Brebeuf, it was as if he didn't feel anything, or, if he did, he did not show it. Somehow he was already in heaven. Heaven is the complete and total identification with him who was martyred for us all.

This door of martyrdom can be illusory, can be a mirage in the desert. One needs great wisdom here. The door *may* open into martyrdom. With this opening will come a mysterious knowledge, which is given to very few: blood shed for God is the cradle of new Christians.

For what else now can save the world? Prayer? Yes. Fasting? Yes. But ultimately only martyrdom can save the world, as it was saved by the Martyr on the Cross. This is why when I cannot sleep at night I walk the desert. I begin to realize that the final stage of my journey lies through that door to martyrdom.

You can open the newspaper today and read about the modern martyrs—in South America, in Russia. When the moment of martyrdom arrives, the souls of men, women, and even children are given by God a new burst of spiritual power. At the one final moment, life surges into a magnificent torrent, the torrent of love. It is the torrent of a goal achieved—martyrdom for the sake of the Beloved.

Many Christians, Jews, Hindus, and Brahmins who have entered into the silence of God have understood this, but how many have *really* entered into the silence of God? How many have touched that silence, have persevered in it, until finally God's silence clothes them with its full radiance?

The heart of man seeks for solutions to his problems until no solutions are left. Then he discovers that the "I" in a sense must disappear, become totally identified with Christ in his silent service to mankind. Yes, there are many silent steps to take before one comes to the door of total identification. But when you arrive there, your heart, like those of the martyrs, will receive a new burst of love, the impulse of a heart which is finally united with the Beloved.

The Song of Songs says, "Do not arouse, do not stir up love" (3:5). Everything is quiet now. Two silences merge into one. The door is open. They who have passed through the door come out on the other side clothed in a mantle of blood. Jesus Christ walks up to them, and welcomes them with outstretched arms. Bloodied and battered, they fall into his arms. New life emanates from them. The mantle of blood is changed into a mantle of gold. Then, ceremoniously, Christ takes their hand and presents them to his Father. His Father rises from his throne and also embraces them. And the Holy Spirit hovers over them with immense joy and gladness.

This is the age of martyrs. Those who are ready for martyrdom must pray for the grace to become martyrs. I have a friend who is a priest; I have known him from his seminary days. He could be called a martyr because he lived in a Japanese prison camp. Three of his confreres had been martyred there. Because God touched his heart, he too now has the desire for martyrdom. I am going to pray for him, pray that he too may some day be a martyr. If he becomes a martyr, he will beget thousands of Christians.

I spoke to God about this. I said, "Do you really want me to pray that people become martyrs—myself and others?" He answered, "Of course you should pray for that. How else is the Church to continue!"

The landscape is flat. It seems to be a desert, but not quite, because all kinds of bushes and flowers angrily snap back at the winds that come at them from all sides. I am alone. I enter the great silence of God, so deep, so still. I see that its depth is really infinite, this great silence of God which is his speech. One does not understand this latter truth right away. A feeling of terrible loneliness takes hold of me, and there is nothing that I can do about it. God seems to have vanished.

I am under one of these angry bushes. I can't find God anywhere except in the midst of the battle between the bush and the wind. But I have entered the great silence of God to be with him, not to get away from him. If the wind is getting stronger, it seems to me that I should seek him in the wind.

Suddenly there is a stillness. I feel I must enter this stillness, but I am reluctant to do so. There are no winds now, but I have decided to follow God wherever he leads. Mine is a simple act. All I have to do is push the bushes aside a little and enter, just as I once stood by the silver sands and entered the sea of infinity. So now I have to enter these bushes.

It is so strange. What shall I find in the heart of the bushes lost in this desert? Slowly, feeling as if each of my arms weighed a thousand pounds, I push the bushes apart and discover a stairway. Slowly, holding onto my cane, I descend into the heart of the bushes.

The steps seemed to have no bottom, going down,

down. On each step I was reminded of a step in the apostolate God had given me. On the first step I found myself walking briskly, happily, with a little attache case and a typewriter. I also had a bag with a few pieces of clothing. I was walking from Isabella Street to Portland Street in Toronto, in the early days of my apostolate.

As I walked, the whole picture of my early poverty and begging arose before my eyes. Another step, and I remembered my involvement in social justice. I looked down and suddenly couldn't see the next step! I had to jump. It was Rochester Street in Ottawa, where I used to get up at 5:30 A.M. and work until 11:00 P.M.

I couldn't see the next few steps either, so I jumped, as if into a void. As I jumped I seemed to soar, and I felt God's hands hold me very gently and place me safely on another step. It was Harlem. It's a long story, the story of my soul and God's love. It's the story of meeting Dorothy Day who came to apologize to me because some of the Catholic Workers didn't recognize me. On another step I met Father Lafarge.

Descending still further, I recalled the tall pines and birches of Combermere, and Bishop William Smith. I am sitting now in the sand by the river, more still than the insects waiting for their prey. They are waiting for their prey; I am listening to the wind in the bushes and talking like this to God.

Don't be astonished, my friends, at this revelry with God. There are fools who talk with God once in a while. I am one of these fools. In Russia we call them *urodivia*, which means fools for Christ's sake. Well, I am one of them. I speak to God in the darkness of the tall pines and the white birches.

Yes, in the midst of that storm, I talked to God and God talked to me. This is what he said:

"Catherine, do you remember your mother's words to you?" I said, "Which, Lord?" "When she said, 'You were born under the shadow of the cross.'" "Oh yes," I said. "I remember that very well." And he said, "That's good, because that is where you are now. All the storms that you have been subjected to were of the Devil. But I am here, and he cannot reach you, because you have passed from the silver sands into the infinity of my silence. Ask me now what you want to know."

"Lord," I said, "it seems incredible that I should be rejected all the time by everybody. You alone know the depth of that rejection. You know what the priests, the nuns, the laity have done to me. I don't know how I have survived. Urodivia, poustinia, sobornost, strannik, molchanie—it just doesn't make sense, Lord."

Very quietly he answered, "It had begun, Catherine, when you were very small. My Father and I and the Holy Spirit hovered over you. At a very young age you fell in love with me. And my mother, whose child you are, was always with you, singing lullabies. You did not understand all that then. I saw the road that you would take, but I could not compel you to take it. It had to be journeyed freely by you.

"Slowly, as the years went by, because you loved me, you followed that path I had arranged for you. Oh, you zigzagged a little when you were young, but then the path straightened out. Now you continue to walk with questions in your mind, but only in your mind. Those questions I can easily answer. Tell me, Catherine, do you love me, my Father, the Holy Spirit, and my mother?"

And when I nodded my head, overwhelmed by what he said, he replied, "That's all that matters. So never be astonished at being rejected and at being whipped and crowned with thorns, and at carrying your cross. Don't be astonished. You want to follow me. You are following me, and I am always nearby."

With these words he put my head on his shoulder, and began patting my hair. Well, I must admit that I was really "out of myself." His hands were calloused but soft, and I let myself go into the arms of God.

✳ The Silence of Old Age

I feel closed in. I have reached the age where people hem me in on all sides. I am not free anymore. I cannot take an airplane and go to Europe if I want to. In many things I cannot dispose of myself. Everything in me seems to be tied up. I walk with small steps. I used to be able to walk out into the woods and see many kinds of landscapes. I roamed up and down mountains and valleys. I was free. But now I feel all bound up. "When you grow old you will stretch out your hands, and somebody else will put a belt around you and take you where you would not go" (John 21: 18). Now I have only one landscape: the heart of God.

But how stupid of me to talk like this, one who has stood at the edge of the silver sands and jumped into the infinity of God's silence. I'm letting the old smother the new. I am losing myself in the past, and God looks at me going over my life. I guess it never occurs to us that tomorrow, or the day after, our steps will falter, that we will be too weak to do this or that. And yet, I think this unfreedom of old age is also an entry into the silence of God.

God offers us many silences—the silence of babyhood, the silence of childhood, the silence of youth and maturity, and finally the silence of old age. My own heart must learn to accept this lack of freedom. People undoubtedly say about me, "Oh well, she is old now. She can't do this and she can't do that." This is good. It is good because then I enter a new depth of silence, the very essence and depth of poverty for which I have so longed. I am now exceedingly free.

"In the past I tried to live, Lord, according to your will. As I bowed my head to your will I lived in this silence of obedience. Your speech, your will, was all light for me, no matter if it was pain or joy. All that came from you was so beautiful, and I felt free. To be in your will, Lord, is to be in your silence, and have a freedom that no one can understand. Then, when I wanted to travel, I would make reservations and go by myself. Now it is no longer so."

But now a new freedom comes to my soul. Yes, I am more bound in some ways, but I am also more free. The earth is becoming a narrow sliver, of no more importance. Heaven is opening before me. This is the goal I always wanted to attain. No wonder earthly landscapes pass out of view. God has given me a new key, and nobody can stop me from entering the landscape of God. Oh, they can herd me into this or that plane, put me into this or that room or motel. But, ah, they cannot tame my wild and immense spirit, which needs no other landscape but the heart of God.

So here we are together, he and I. He is bound too. Bound with nails. They hurt much more than the soft bandages they use on me. Then again, perhaps he does the binding so as to keep me close to him. Little do they know that when they bind me, a window is always left open, and I go and lose myself in God.

Yes, as I prayed today I saw that the Lord had removed all scenery, all earthly panoramas, and given me a new panorama, new scenery—himself. Previously, I had been traveling over seas and mountains and deserts. Today I entered the immense scenery of God's own heart. My whole life, from babyhood until now, passed before me.

Russian babies were always bound up in swaddling clothes by their nurses or mothers. I don't ever remember the joy of having free limbs as a baby. Mine were always bound. Then one day the Lord touched me, as if with a wand, and I became free of the bonds. My baby clothes fell off and I found myself pumping my little legs—happy, gurgling, all excited. Whoever it was who had bound me had gone away, and I was delighted.

My parents allowed me to be free, but within a strict discipline of love and understanding. I was never free as people are here, to do whatever they want, when they want, as they want. No, there were always boundaries.

I remember when I was about two years old, I was put in a harness and made to walk. So I was more free, but still in the power of my mother or father. All during my growing up, I became more free, but never completely free from bonds. I fell in love with God, and when you are in love with God, there is full freedom, provided you do what he wants you to do. Thus, surrounding me all my life was this strange lack of freedom on the one hand, and a total freedom on the other. At one and the same time I grew up in the midst of a total discipline and a total freedom.

Then came my marriage and the war. I passed from the simple life of a child to that of a young adult, and thence to the life of an older person who submitted herself voluntarily to the discipline of God, as expressed by people in charge of me in one way or another. I was in love with God. And under the discipline of my parents and of the Church, I was tremendously free.

I would have to say that, in general, I was an exceedingly obedient person. The landscape I walked in this early part of my life was simple, ordinary, gray, with a few flowers strewn along the way. Obedience gives birth to flowers for those who walk in her path. Oh, I wasn't perfectly obedient. Far from it! But nevertheless, I can say that I was an obedient person.

Now I have reached my eighties. People in their eighties usually are not obedient to anyone! Such people usually demand obedience from others. But I don't feel like that. I feel that obedience is still at my side. I feel that I am under the supreme obedience of the Lord.

I feel I have finally attained poverty, the kind I have always dreamed about. My time now is God's time. I have an intense desire to pray, and to fast. But I know that neither fasting nor prayer is the most important thing, but rather to *be a prayer*, and to go about the world doing good to mankind as long as I possibly can, as long as my fingers can move and my mind is clear.

Thus, while I feel bound by my lack of freedom in my old age (something like the swaddling clothes I had on as a baby), I am beginning to realize that all these things are being done by God. He looked down on me and still saw a lot of insects that needed to be killed—the insect of pride, the insect of desiring to be free in the wrong way. Suddenly, he put his hand on all these insects and they died.

Who are these people binding me? Everybody in the apostolate. Oh yes, they are doing it out of love, but it is still hard.

Father Briere often did the actual "binding," with airplanes, accommodations and such. But I never considered him as a "binder." He has been very kind to me all through these years. He always consulted me regarding all these things, understanding that it is not easy to be bound in your old age. He was always so very kind and gentle and tender.

I feel very happy when he is around and thank God for him. I could not deny that he is also part of the bandages that bind me, but they are bandages with which I need to be bound. Thus it is that the Lord prepares the infant in her old age to enter the kingdom of heaven!

I am lost in the tenderness of God. It is a very wonderful thing that a human being can be filled, encompassed by, replenished with the tenderness of God. His tenderness is always there. But there are so many other things that draw our attention away from God that his tenderness towards us often passes unnoticed.

When you have entered the *great silence of God*, everything changes. All the things that mattered yesterday do not seem to matter so much today. In fact, one looks for a moment at yesterday and wonders how it was possible that our attention could focus so absorbingly on the utterly unimportant things that make up the warp and woof of our lives.

Now, clothed with the patience which is part of God's love for us, we sit very still. On the table lies the wool of our lives, as it were, which seemed so important. Here, on this corner of the table, lies death. All our lives we were so afraid of it. But why? Probably because most people consider it to be the end. For these people, the fear of death is overwhelming. The fact that we shall lose our hold on existence such as we know it terrifies us. This is how it is for the majority. But for the few who warmed their souls on the silver sands, and plunged into the infinity of God's immense sea of silence, it is like that no longer.

The Lord wanted us to love as he loved, so he made us his children and heirs. To those who really wanted to see with the eyes of faith, he revealed the truth about death. Physical death is not the end. We shall, after death, enter into true life, eternity, where we can really be ourselves, instead of forever using masks to hide our real faces.

How sad are those masks you see in coffins! Perhaps sometime before death, for one fleeting moment, each person cried out, "Why did I use this mask instead of being myself? Why did I not reveal that which should have been revealed? Why did I hide what never should have been hidden?" Then, on this last thought, the eyes closed in death.

There is a moment when God gives us a key to the mystery of life. We always had a key to his heart, and he always had a key to our hearts. But this is a special key. It is the key of *wisdom*, which allows us to live a good life. It is given to those who have walked the silver sands and, out of love for him, decided to plunge into the endless infinity of his sea of silence. They needed the key to guide themselves amid the noises of the world. They needed a key to choose what is wise.

One of the things that Satan does is confuse. And his favorite confusion is to substitute earthly wisdom for divine wisdom. Many are caught on this bait. But with the key of wisdom one can avoid such pitfalls. And this key can unlock many doors, even doors men have invented that block their own true progress. Evil and madness have taken hold of them.

When you die, this key will die with you; no one who is looking through your effects will ever find it. Now it is no longer necessary for you. But throughout your life it is a wonderful guide. Hold on to it! As I said, this key of wisdom is given to those who have plunged into the infinity of God's silence. Or, to put it another way, it is given to children. Only children can possess this key. "Grown-ups" cannot hold onto it. They let it slip through their fingers. Their intelligence stands in the way of the simplicity necessary to use the key. Children know how to play with this key, and, as they do, their knowledge grows. They might be "children" with white beards and white hair. Nevertheless, they know something which very few people know: besides having penetrated the infinite sea of God's silence, they now belong to the kingdom as "little children."

And so, after you enter the silence of God, the most marvelous thing begins to happen, impossible to describe. There are no words to express the beauty, joy, and pain of this experience. It is as if one were already in the parousia!

For a second, there is a backward glance at the kenosis through which you have passed. Now you notice that it was a complete emptying of yourself. The false self seems never to have existed. The kenosis seems so small a price for all that God has done for you. The whole of your life now falls into two parts: the kenosis, the time of pain and problems, and the time of childhood, when you began to understand God's speech, when your mind and heart and soul became wide open to his Word. The key has done its work. You know now, almost without knowing, that you are wise, and that this wisdom will grow in you, for you have the key to all its chambers.

There is a wonderful relaxation of soul and a patience that enters one's being. There is greater understanding. For having become possessed of the key of wisdom, you now "see" without seeing, and "hear" without hearing. It seems you have touched something like the hem of the Father's garment.

At this juncture you seem to pass out of yourself. It is not a question of dangling between heaven and earth. Rather, it's as if an immense hand enfolded you gently and lifted you higher and higher. You are able to hear a choir of angels singing to a Child, singing with joy, and you become part of this rejoicing.

Then, peacefully, someone puts you in your bed. The angelic choir ceases. A beautiful voice begins to sing a lullaby. All this is what happens when you accept the key of wisdom. He who plunges lovingly into the infinite sea of God's silence, and opens its treasures with the key of wisdom, has finally reached the goal. But the goal is a cross, and in the distance one hears men selecting nails.

The goal is the cross because the key of wsdom gives a power to look into men's hearts. They come before me, one after the other, and they ask questions. They demand answers. They crowd around me in an ever-increasing throng. They cry out for me to be an intercessor between them and God. I do not quite understand it all— partly because they speak so rapidly. They look sickly and miserable.

I see that they are all tied up with strings of different colors. One is pink and reddish—human respect. Another is green—envy, the desire to be better than others. Others are tied with white string. One would imagine that this color is symbolic of childlike innocence. But no! It is the drab, grayish white of indifference. They are all wrapped up in themselves, living for themselves and no one else. They are indifferent to God, to love, to anything that really matters. There are other colors as well, symbolizing the seven capital sins, which impede the growth of the soul.

I hold the key of wisdom in my hands. I look at it and I ask God if he really wishes me to have it. For by giving it to me he inflicts deep sorrow on my soul. He answers very simply, "You wished to follow me, so now you are. That is what I see, the souls of men. I am showing you the depth of degradation in man that brings forth tears from my Father's eyes."

I hear these words of his and I begin to cry. I kneel down and put my face into his lap. I cannot stop crying. His hand is over my head and he strokes my hair and says, "Those who want to follow me totally have to be total. Catherine, do you know what it means to be total? It means complete self-emptying. It means crucifixion, but it also means resurrection. Always, always, every hour of every day, you have a choice—to accept or reject. So far you have accepted to follow me totally. It is up to you to continue. My Father and I and the Holy Spirit give you complete freedom to reject or to accept us, remember that."

So I look again at the key, and at the people clamoring for answers. I realize, with a new understanding, that there is only one way that I can bring the peace of God to these people, and that is face to face, person to person. Mass meetings are of no avail. Lectures and speeches given there pass in one ear and out of the other and are soon forgotten. There may be a few exceptions. There is only one way to bring men to God and that is to love each individual personally.

Loving does not necessarity mean liking. But still it is loving, yes—totally, completely, utterly. Take the key of wisdom and unlock your own heart. Then let people in, one by one. Listen to them with full attention, with all your mind, heart, soul and body, unto exhaustion. And look!—the exhaustion will be lifted, and you will be able to listen still more. Yes, love must be communicated person to person; otherwise it will not be effective.

✳ The End of All Waiting

It is impossible to convey to anybody what waiting on God or waiting for God means. Of course, God is always present; God is always "with us." He is always "coming" to us, but we are not always awaiting his arrival.

There is a kind of waiting that is anxious. Take the parable of the workers in the vineyard. The owner comes several times and finds out that there are still people who have not been hired. I call them "the waiting people," because they were waiting to be hired. This is not the kind of waiting I am talking about. These people were excited, annoyed, and depressed. They had all kinds of emotions that are incompatible with the silence of God. Only in a wide sense can we say that they were waiting for God.

No, real waiting is quite different. It is quiet, peaceful, waiting for God to do something, but you really don't know exactly what. There is immense joy in your heart. This kind of waiting is something like waiting for a loved one to arrive. Lovers pace back and forth when the beloved is even fifteen minutes late. They are nervous, excited, but out of love and concern for the beloved.

But waiting for God isn't *exactly* like this. I would call waiting for God tranquillity, a certain tranquillity that takes hold of you entirely, so that nothing stirs within you. There is only one thought: "He will come in his own time." It is a kind of totality of peace.

All is quiet in one's heart. The mind is asleep but the heart is receptive. All emotions are subdued except the powerful emotion of love. Love is in one's heart, as it should have been in Eve's heart. She should have taken the apple and thrown it away. Then she would have known true freedom.

In this waiting for God, everything is at peace. The totality of the person is at peace, waiting. And, if you are in this state of peace, God allows you to see why other people are not at peace, why there are so many problems. All the "whys" in the world seem to flash in front of you like a movie, but this does not disturb one iota of your own peace. Rather, the "whys" incite you to pray for others and for their problems.

This peace, like a shield, surrounds me. It protects me from everything that could hurt or upset me. It is the peace of waiting. Don't ever lose this immense peace of waiting on and for the Lord. I wish that I could convey some of it through my writings, through my lectures, through any means of communication whatsoever. But all means of communication have proved useless for this.

God has set us aside and given us his own patience to wait on him, to be ready for his coming. Do not be disturbed. The exact hour and minute of his coming lies in his hand and in the love of his heart. My task, your task, is only to wait without emotional storms, without impatience, without any pacing up and down. No. There is only the totality of the person always expecting the footsteps of the Lord.

I wish, as I said, that I could convey something of the peacefulness, the patience, the prayerfulness which comes from my own heart as one who has stood for a while on the silver sands and plunged into the sea of the infinity of the Lord. I wish I could convey it, but it is impossible. All I can say is, "It is so."

Then, at a certain time, the Lord comes, bounding over the mountains like a person in love: "Hark! My lover—here he comes, springing across the mountains, leaping across the hills" (Song of Songs 2:8). Of course, this is poetic language; yet it is the true language of love. Other poets have tried to put into words the experience of the Lord's coming—Francis Thompson, for example, in *The Hound of Heaven*:

> "All which I took from thee I did but take,
> Not for thy harms,
> But just that thou might'st seek it in My arms.
> All which thy child's mistake
> Fancies as lost, I have stored for thee at home:
> Rise, clasp My hand, and come."

> Halts by me that footfall:
> Is my gloom, after all,
> Shade of His hand, outstretched caressingly?
> "Ah, fondest, blindest, weakest,
> I am He whom thou seekest!
> Thou dravest love from thee, who dravest Me."*

---

*Francis Thompson, *The Hound of Heaven* (Oxford: A.R. Mowbray & Co., 1947), pp. 26 and 28.

Yes, magnificent poetry, but even this falls short of expressing what happens at the Lord's coming. There are no adequate words to express the moment of the Beloved's arrival.

There is no landscape now. All around me is fire. I walk amid this fire as if compelled to do so. I seek to understand why. Why have all the landscapes disappeared, and why am I now in the midst of these flames? They raise me higher and higher, but I do not see where I am going. I am beyond the earth now, beyond the planets.

A beautifully wrought chalice is placed into my hands. I look at it and its beauty overwhelms me. I either swoon or fall asleep. I am totally unaware of what is happening, except for one thing—that I am following God, somehow entering into the heart of God.

In another hand I am holding a staff, wonderfully carved, but without any precious stones. It is the staff of a poor shepherd. Staff in one hand, chalice in the other, I rise higher and higher. I look down at my naked feet and notice that I am actually walking on a staircase of fire. The flames lick my feet without burning them. From seemingly far away, and yet ever so close, a voice says to me, "Higher, friend, come up higher."

Again, it is beyond my understanding. "Lord, what do you mean? How can I walk through fire and not be burned? I don't understand."

A voice answers, "Understanding! You don't need understanding. Turn around." I turn around and look back down the fiery staircase I ascended and upon which I am still walking. I have left understanding far behind, on one of the stairs. Wisdom too is behind me, though not as far away as understanding. Hope is my sole companion, here with me at my side. It looks like water, like pure crystal. People seem to approach me with all kinds of vessels, to fill them with the hope that seems to flow from me. I begin to feel the presence of someone so beautiful and powerful that I want to embrace him; but he seems always a few fiery steps in front of me.

I am holding the chalice from which the water is flowing. I notice that the feet of the people who are coming to drink from the chalice are not burnt either. They do not seem to notice that there is this fire all around me that continues to lift me towards the summit of some mountain I am supposed to climb.

I see that the chalice is overflowing. From it people are drinking water and wine. This water and wine seemed to come from me, but I see now they do not. They come from God. I stand in the middle of this fiery staircase and cannot go any further. I see that the chalice not only has water and wine in it, but bread as well. And hungry and thirsty people continue to come and be fed.

A voice says to me, "Let them drink and eat." I do. The chalice remains full. Slowly, with a clarity of vision I never possessed in my life, I begin to understand what is happening to me. I begin to see the reason for my existence. But the fiery staircase is still there, and I continue.

The extraordinary thing about the fire which surrounds me is that it brings me great joy. Now, in the midst of this fire, I see a tree. I continue to hold the chalice in one hand and the staff in the other. People continue to come and drink the water and wine and eat the bread. Surrounded by the flames, which do not hurt me, I watch the tree of faith grow and grow.

The fire begins to recede a little bit, enough for me to

lie down and rest in the immense shade of the tree of faith. So I sit down with my back against the soft and tender core of the tree. It seems that I forget everything that ever was, and yet I remember everything that ever was. I recognize not only hope by my side, but love as well; both of them have grown to immense proportions.

A voice speaks: "This is your life of hope and love. Now give me the chalice and set down the staff."

In the midst of that fiery landscape, filled with the most beautiful singing I have ever heard, I see two hands take the chalice, which is very heavy. (I wonder how I carried it so far.) One hand holds the chalice, and the other falls to the side of a man. He comes near me and says gently and tenderly, "Drink," and so I drink.

The last thing I see is that the hand which was at his side, and the hand which offered me the chalice, were both pierced. I say, "Your hands have been pierced." And the voice becomes even more tender and says, "Yes, for you and for all mankind. Now come and drink what remains in the chalice. Then come and rest your head upon my heart."

I do as I have been told. Then I know what very few people know—ecstasy.

Again, the landscape with which I began—the silver sands and the infinite sea of God's love and silence—appears. It is the same and yet different. This time I come across a small village. It is Nazareth, and I am there like one seeking a lost treasure. I sit down beside a little pond where people are coming to wash their laundry. I do not understand why I am suddenly in such a poor and humble place. I am bewildered, for I am seeking the great silence of God.

The place is fairly noisy. I cannot find God or his silence. Where is it? What has happened to it? Where did it go? I am very tired. So I find some shade and fall asleep. But the sleep is not restful. I am restless; my heart is tortured and cries out, "God, where are you? I want you now, for I have made this long journey. I want to rest in your silence, my Lord."

Suddenly I am awake. The road is dusty but I follow it. When you are seeking, one road seems as good as another. There is a strange beauty about the road, but somehow I am not able to see it.

Then, from around a bend in the road, a young woman walks towards me. I stop, and she stops too. We stand facing one another. I say to her, "You are the one I am seeking. You can lead me to my Love. I want to speak with him. I believe that the only way I can speak with him is by silence. The further I walk into his silence, the more I have been able to hear his voice."

She looks at me with a lovely gentleness. There is a stone nearby. She points to it and says, "Come, sit down here with me. Yes, you have found me. I truly am the gate that leads to him whom you love. Sit down here. Hold my hand. I shall become a gate for you to pass through. I am the woman wrapped in the silence of God."

She opened her arms, which were covered with a black mantle. But when she opened it, the inside was all crimson red. She was the spouse of the Holy Spirit. Without hesitation I walked into her heart. And in this immense heart of the woman who is the Mother of God and Mother of men, I met him whom I love.

Pax Caritas

I am a woman
      wrapped in
      Silence too.
For silence has become
      attire and song!
Silence is golden
      with light exploding
      as you become one with God
      and so do I.

            I am a woman
                  wrapped in silence too.
            Silence has become
                  for me
            Attire and song.